MW01097921

THE MOFFAT TUNNEL

A Brief History

By

Charles Albi and Kenton Forrest

ACKNOWLEDGMENTS

We are deeply indebted to the following individuals whose generous assistance made the completion of this history an easier task than it otherwise might have been: the Moffat Tunnel Commissioners who gave us unlimited access to their files; Roseanne Ball, secretary to the commission who helped with our research in those files; A. D. Mastrogiuseppe, Jr. at the Western History Department of the Denver Public Library; and Richard H. Kindig, who not only read the manuscript and provided some of his own photographs but aided us in selection of photographs from the Otto C. Perry collection. Other pictorial assistance came from Ted Benson, Mike Danneman, Ronald C. Hill, Mrs. Louis A. Larsen, Mel Patrick, Steve Patterson, Robert W. Richardson, Elmer Schlotz, F. Hol Wagner, Jr., the public relation staff of Burlington Northern, Inc., and Don Snoddy and William Kratville of the Union Pacific Railroad Museum. Bruce Hogue edited the original manuscript, and Marjorie Forrest provide both editorial and typing skills. Helen H. Albi assisted with proof reading, and William C. Jones was helpful in various ways. In 2002, Robert Jensen designed the revised edition, and Pete Aldrich typed additional captions.

© 2002 by Colorado Railroad Historical Foundation, Inc. No part of this book may be reproduced without prior written authorization of the publisher, other than brief excerpts embodied in critical reviews.

Fifth printing [revised] 2002

ISBN 0-918654-26-2

COLORADO RAILROAD MUSEUM
P. O. Box 10
Golden, Colorado 80402-0010

Thru
The Moffat Tunnel

Reduced fare of $5.00 for the round trip in effect every Sunday—Denver to Tabernash, via the Moffat Tunnel.

Leave Denver 8:40 A. M.
Returning, Arrive Denver 5:45 P. M.

For Information, Call

MAIN 3262

The Denver & Salt Lake Ry. Co.

F. J. TONER,
Traffic Manager

While its east portal resembles a mighty fortress, compared with the mountains of the Continental Divide even such a huge project as the Moffat Tunnel appears small. The level area in the foreground is composed of rock excavated during construction. (L.C. McClure photo, CRRM collection)

(*title page*) Perhaps no other photograph more dramatically symbolizes the conquest of the Continental Divide than this one of the Denver & Salt Lake Mallet 205 entering the West Portal on opening day, February 26, 1928. (Western History Collection, Denver Public Library)

THE MOFFAT TUNNEL
A Brief History

In the fall of 1866 the Union Pacific Railroad had reached the point in the construction of its transcontinental line where a final decision had to be made in the selection of a route across the Continental Divide. Hoping to run its line through Denver, Union Pacific's chief engineer, General Grenville M. Dodge, had three Rocky Mountain passes under serious consideration: Berthoud, at the head of Clear Creek; Boulder, or Rollins as it was then coming to be known, above South Boulder Creek and Cache la Poudre, far to the north. The general himself barely escaped being trapped by a sudden blizzard while exploring the high reaches of Rollins Pass that November. This experience convinced him that any route through the high Rockies west of Denver would be impractical to build and operate, and Union Pacific followed the easier grades of southern Wyoming. For the next seven decades, Denver and Colorado were relegated to the backwaters of transcontinental commerce.

There was, however, one man whose destiny became a lifelong project to remedy this situation. David Halliday Moffat, Jr. had been born in the Hudson Valley of New York in 1839. He began his career as a bank teller in New York City but soon moved west, first to Des Moines, Iowa, and shortly to Omaha, where by his twenty-first birthday he had become a "paper" millionaire dealing in real estate. Within a few months he continued his westward migration, opening a bookstore in Denver in the spring of 1860. When the Union Pacific made its decision to bypass the city, Dave Moffat was cashier of the First National Bank and one of the community's established leaders. Although he was to build his fortune in banking and mining, Moffat was destined to be remembered in history because of his involvement with most of the important railroads built in Colorado. He served as treasurer of the Denver Pacific Railroad & Telegraph Company, the first line to reach the city from the Union Pacific at Cheyenne, Wyoming, in 1870. With Governor John Evans he incorporated the narrow gauge Denver South Park & Pacific and soon became receiver of W.A.H. Loveland's Colorado Central, the first company to lay rails into the mountains west of Denver.

David Moffat relaxes at his desk at some time during the years when he was building his Denver Northwestern & Pacific Railway across the roof of the continent. (Denver Public Library Western History Department)

EARLY ATTEMPTS TO PENETRATE THE DIVIDE

In 1881, Moffat's name appeared as one the backers of the Denver Utah & Pacific, a narrow gauge line projected up South Boulder Canyon, through a tunnel at Rollins Pass, and on to a connection with the Rio Grande Western in Utah. Moffat and his associates shortly sold the DU&P to the Burlington, which had just completed its line into Denver from the east, expecting that this road would build a standard gauge railroad through the mountains. However, the Burlington was unable to locate a feasible route over the divide and, beset with other problems, soon abandoned the project. In the spring of 1883, General William Jackson Palmer's Denver & Rio Grande, in connection with the Rio Grande Western in Utah, actually completed the first rail line through the Rocky Mountains to Salt Lake City, although the tracks were narrow gauge and followed a circuitous route via the Royal Gorge and Marshall Pass.

In that same year the Colorado Midland, under the leadership of James J. Hagerman, commenced building a standard gauge railroad west from Colorado Springs. Spurred by this new competition and also realizing the ultimate shortcoming of its narrow gauge track, D&RG began to widen its gauge and to build an improved main line west via Tennessee Pass near Leadville. Moffat become president of the Rio Grande in

3

The Moffat Depot at 15th and Bassett Streets in Denver is seen shortly before the 1947 demise of the Denver & Salt Lake Railway. The head house still exists, although its interior has suffered severe fire damage. (Lad Arend photo, CRRM collection)

late 1885, and both he and Palmer felt the importance of renewing the effort to find a direct route west of Denver. Unfortunately, thorough surveys of the entire divide failed to reveal a practical route and D&RG directors in New York City could not be persuaded to put more money into the project. For this and for other differences in opinion, Moffat was removed as president of the road in 1891.

During the last decade of the 19th century, Moffat spent much time in New York and traveling in Europe, and his interest in his railroad project seemingly waned. The concept of a tunnel under the Continental Divide was kept alive by an unlikely promotional scheme known as the Atlantic and Pacific Tunnel, to be built above Georgetown under Loveland Pass. Many investors were enticed by the hope of great wealth that would be gained from minerals to be found in the tunnel excavation and from rentals charged the associated Denver

Apex & Western Railroad. Backed by H.A.W. Tabor, some construction was accomplished, but the project had fizzled by 1898.

Two years later, Moffat reappeared with W. G. Evans as a backer of the Denver & Northwestern Railway, an electric line to be built in sections to Salt Lake City with each part to be constructed as the preceding section became profitable. Electric railways were then being built in all parts of the country, and both men were major stockholders in the Denver Tramway, which operated that city's electric street railway system. However, this plan soon appeared to Moffat to be a poor substitute for his dream of a standard gauge railroad to the Pacific, and the D&NW was completed only as a narrow gauge interurban line to Golden and the Leyden coal mines.

THE MOFFAT ROAD

Finally, in early 1902 David Moffat announced his momentous decision: "I have decided to build a steam railroad from Denver to Salt Lake City." He was 63 years old and realized that time was running out for him to fulfill his ambition. The Denver Northwestern & Pacific Railway was incorporated on July 18, 1902, with William G. Evans, Walter S. Cheesman, and Charles J. Hughes, Jr. among the principal investors along with Moffat.

The heroic story of David Moffat's struggle to build his railroad, virtually with no outside assistance, is well known to students of western history. The opposition of man and nature worked against him at every turn. Little financial assistance was forthcoming from his associates in Denver, and the Union Pacific in the person of E. H. Harriman saw to it that there would be no sources of money in New York. Attempts to raise capital

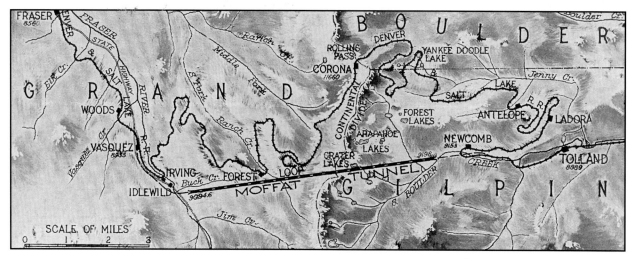

(Moffat Tunnel Commission)

For nearly a quarter century of long winters it was necessary for two rotary snow plows to continually shuttle over Rollins Pass in order to keep the railroad open above timberline. (CRRM collection)

in Europe proved fruitless. Consequently, Moffat's only recourse was to consume his entire personal fortune in building his line to the Yampa coal fields in northwestern Colorado, the first source of any appreciable revenue.

He was fortunate in gaining the services of a brilliant locating engineer, H. A. Sumner. While prior attempts in building a railroad up South Boulder Canyon had failed due to the stream bed rising at a rate with which the railroad grade could not keep pace, Sumner ran the line of the DNW&P up the rise of the Leyden Mesa northwest of Denver. He was able to gain elevation and maintain a steady two percent grade by a spectacular double reverse curve at the head of the mesa. After a series of tunnels north of Coal Creek, Sumner's survey entered the canyon at a point high above the stream bed, which the two percent grade did not reach until the town of Pinecliff. Drilling the 30 tunnels along this route required the largest order of black powder placed in Colorado up to that time.

Sumner then proceeded with the "temporary" line over Rollins Pass. Doubling the grade to four percent above the location of the originally proposed 2.6-mile main range tunnel, he achieved Middle Park via a spectacular route above timberline and the highest railroad pass on the North American Continent at 11,660 feet above sea level.

Almost immediately, Rollins Pass brought fame to the Moffat Road as one of the most popular scenic railroad trips in a state already boasting of many spectacular routes. The Moffat Road fully exploited the benefits of taking a trip to "the top of the world." In the years before the family automobile, not only were the regular passenger trains filled, but many specials ran on Sundays and holidays. Fishing and hunting in the virgin territory served by the railroad acted as further lures for passenger

traffic. The railroad even capitalized on one of its greatest enemies, the weather, by bringing carloads of snow to Denver in June and July. The general passenger agents of Colorado railroads at the turn of the century missed few chances to bring attention to their various lines in the heated competition for tourist patronage.

By 1907, rails had been extended on through Middle Park to Kremmling, where another obstacle loomed. Gore Canyon, the only feasible route to the west, had been usurped by the United States Department of the Interior as a reservoir site. After much legal maneuvering, during which it developed that the power company proposing to build the dam was supported by E. H. Harriman, President Theodore Roosevelt brought his influence to the side of those wishing the canyon to be used as a railroad route, and the dispute was settled. Moffat pushed his rails on to Steamboat Springs by 1911, but the line through Gore Canyon and over the divide to Yampa Valley involved extremely difficult construction. Although he was reputed to be the wealthiest man in Colorado just ten years earlier, Moffat's funds were exhausted. While in New York City attempting to raise money to build his tunnel and extend his railroad westward, he died on March 18, 1911.

The railroad soon fell into receivership, emerging in 1913 as the Denver & Salt Lake Railroad under the leadership of Charles Boettcher and Moffat's old associate, Gerald Hughes, with Newman Erb as president. Although David Moffat had died with his dream unfulfilled, the spirit of his project lived on with his associates and the those who had worked for him.

The railroad was finally extended to Craig in 1913, and this turned out to be the end of the line. The tremendous cost of operating over Rollins Pass consumed each year's profit. The track was subject to snow blockades from September through June and was frequently closed for weeks at a time. In 1917, the hapless railroad again fell into receivership under Boettcher and W. R. Freeman. The only hope of completing the line and making it a viable force in developing the territory it served lay in construction of the main range tunnel, but as long as the operation of the route over the pass consumed all profits there were no funds available for the project.

The first hope of breaking this dilemma arose in late 1920. The valuable service of the Moffat Road during World War I in transporting coal and oil from northwestern Colorado had emphasized the line's importance to the people of the state. Denver backers of the tunnel project had quite a bit of political skill. At two points in southern Colorado, Monarch Pass and Cumbres Pass, it had long been felt that tunneling would be of great benefit to areas on the Western Slope. Therefore, the Tri-Tunnel Bill was introduced in the state legislature to provide public financial support for building the two southern tunnels as well as the Moffat. Unfortunately, political interests in the southern and southwestern parts of the state were unhappy at the prospect that Denver might gain any advantage from the proposal and voted it down. Eventually their scheme backfired, since Denver was able to finance its own tunnel, while the other areas were never able to raise the money needed to complete their proposed bores.

BUILDING THE
MAIN RANGE TUNNEL

Ironically, Mother Nature, that old enemy of the Moffat, finally provided the means for overcoming the opposition to state financial support for construction of the Moffat Tunnel. On the evening of June 3, 1921, a devastating flood caused by heavy rains in the upper Arkansas River Valley destroyed the central business district of Pueblo, resulting in over $16,000,000 property damage and the deaths of more than 100 persons. The citizens of Pueblo immediately sought state funds to build flood control facilities that would insure against the repetition of such a disaster. Moffat Tunnel advocates at once saw an unequaled opportunity to gain the approval of southern Colorado voters for the tunnel, and on April 8, 1922, Governor Oliver H. Shoup called a special session of the state legislature to consider funding the two projects. Under the leadership of William G. Evans, support was rallied for the Moffat Tunnel bill, and on April 29 the measure passed, along with the Pueblo Flood Conservancy bill. After sixty long years, David Moffat's dream was about to be realized.

The Moffat Tunnel Improvement District was established, including within its boundaries the City and County of Denver and all or part of each county served by the Denver & Salt Lake Railway, with the authority to levy taxes and issue bonds secured by real estate within the district. Governor Shoup named as the original Moffat Tunnel Commissioners William P. Robinson, Charles MacAllister Willcox, and W. N. W. Blayney of Denver; Charles H. Leckenby of Steamboat Springs, and Charles H. Wheeler of Yampa. To determine the legality of the legislation, a friendly suit was filed in the district court in Golden, Jefferson County, in July. This set into motion a series of legal procedures that worked their way through the court system with almost unheard of speed, and on June 11, 1923, the United States Supreme Court affirmed the vital point in question—the legality of using public money to support a private enterprise. Within two weeks the initial bond issue of $6,720,000 was sold and construction was ready to begin.

SLEEPING CAR SERVICE ON TRAINS 1 AND 2	TRAIN No. 1 STOPS AT PHIPPSBURG FOR BREAKFAST	No. 3 DAILY Scenic Special	No. 1 Mail and Expr. Daily	Eleva-tion	"THE MOFFAT ROAD" TIME TABLE STATIONS		Miles	No. 2 Mail and Expr. Daily	No. 4 DAILY Scenic Special	PARLOR CAR SERVICE ON TRAINS 3 AND 4
		AM	PM					AM	PM	
		8 45	8 30	5,170	Lv.........DENVER.........Ar		0	7 45	5 45	
		9 00	8 44	5,215	"......Utah Junction......Lv		3	7 31	5 31	
		9 06	f 8 54	5,268	"........Ralston........ "		7	f 7 23	f 5 23	
		9 17	f 9 08	5,687	"....Leyden Junction.... "		13	f 7 10	f 5 10	
		9 28	f 9 20	6,162	"........Arena........ "		18	f 6 57	f 4 57	
		9 43	f 9 45	6,783	"......Plainview...... "		24	f 6 42	f 4 42	
		9 51	f 9 56	7,040	"........Scenic........ "		27	f 6 34	f 4 34	
		10 01	f10 09	7,457	"......Crescent...... "		32	f 6 20	f 4 20	
		f10 05	f10 13	7,650	"......Miramonte...... "		34	f 6 14	f 4 14	
		10 17	10 30	7,958	"......Pine Cliff...... "		37	6 04	4 04	
		10 27	10 45	8,367	"......ROLLINSVILLE...... "		42	5 50	3 50	
		10 42	11 02	8,889	"........TOLLAND........ "		47	5 35	3 35	
		10 49	11 15	9,153	"....Newcomb (East Portal).... "		50	5 15	3 21	
		10 59	f11 25	9,380	"........Dora........ "		52	f 5 07	f 3 17	
				10,700	"....Yankee Doodle Lake.... "		60			
		11 37	f12 15	10,860	"......Dixie Lake...... "		61	f 4 35	f 2 45	
		11 59	12 40	11,660	Ar }......CORONA......{ Lv		65	4 15	2 30	
			12 45	11,660	Lv }..."TOP O' THE WORLD"...{ Ar		65	4 10		
			f12 59	10,980	"........Loop........Lv		69	f 3 44		
			f 1 25	9,585	"........ARROW........ "		76	f 2 54		
			1 50	8,950	"....Irvings (West Portal).... "		80	2 35		
			f 1 52	8,935	"......Vasquez...... "		81	f 2 22		
			2 10	8,560	"........FRASER........ "		85	2 10		
			2 20	8,310	Ar }......TABERNASH......{ Lv		89	2 00		
			2 30	8,310	Lv }......TABERNASH......{ Ar		89	1 50		
			f 2 41	8,150	"......Elkdale......Lv		93	f 1 39		
			2 57	7,935	"........GRANBY........ "		99	1 27		
			3 25	7,665	"......SULPHUR SPRINGS...... "		109	1 03		
			....	7,635	"......Byers Canon...... "		110	....		
			3 40	7,595	"........Dollofs........ "		113			
			f 3 56	7,345	"......Parshall...... "		114	12 46		
			4 15	7,322	"......Troublesome...... "		121	12 26		
				7,321	"......KREMMLING...... "		126	12 12		
			4 51	6,881	"......Gore Canon...... "		130	....		
			5 20	6,728	"........Radium........ "		139	11 30		
			f 5 27	6,700	"......State Bridge...... "		149	11 05		
			5 48	7,210	"......Orestod...... "		151	f10 59		
			f 6 18	7,805	"........McCOY........ "		157	10 43		
			6 46	8,252	"......Volcano...... "		166	f10 16		
			7 05	7,884	"......Toponas...... "		176	9 50		
			7 20	7,430	Ar }......YAMPA......{ Lv		185	9 30		
			7 45	7,430	Lv }......PHIPPSBURG......{ Ar		191	9 10		
			8 05	7,401	"......PHIPPSBURG...... "		191	9 00		
			f 8 08	7,355	"........OAK CREEK........ "		194	8 45		
			8 14	7,215	"........Oak Hills........ "		195	f 8 39		
			8 37	6,830	"........Haybro........ "		198	8 33		
			9 00	6,680	"........Sidney........ "		207	8 10		
			f 9 17	6,526	"......STEAMBOAT SPRINGS...... "		214	7 50		
			9 26	6,477	"......Brookston...... "		221	f 7 30		
			f........	6,447	"........Milner........ "		224	7 22		
			f 9 38	6,425	"......Tow Creek...... "		227	f........		
			9 45	6,408	"........BEAR RIVER........ "		229	f 7 09		
			10 10	6,330	"......MT. HARRIS...... "		231	7 05		
			10 23	6,278	"........HAYDEN........ "		238	6 47		
			10 55	6,175	"......Cary Ranch...... "		242	6 33		
			AM		Ar.........CRAIG.........Lv		255	6 00 PM		

Train stops on signal.

This June 10, 1927, Denver & Salt Lake timetable shows the final schedules on the old Rollins Pass line before the tunnel was completed. (Denver Public Library Western History Department)

The contract was awarded to Hitchcock & Tinkler, a firm that had done much previous work for the Moffat Road. The commission had made a tunnel survey the previous year, but the west portal was moved 400 feet to the south of the original location because geologists said that this would provide excavation through more solid rock. A good deal of survey work was done at night, with powerful lights at both portals and at the mountain summit being used as targets. The pioneer bore method of construction was used, with the smaller tunnel allowing crosscuts to be made to the main tunnel, thus speeding work as several headings could be worked simultaneously. The pioneer tunnel would eventually be used to transport Western Slope water into the Denver system, a concept which had been instrumental in passing the tunnel legislation.

Construction camps were established at both portals. These were self contained communities complete with schools, hospitals, housing, and recreation facilities. Although there was some problem with gambling and bootleg liquor, the camps were remarkably free from the frontier atmosphere that might have been expected. The morale of the work force was generally high, due to relatively good pay for the time (an average of $5.15 for an eight-hour shift) and the attention of the contractors to safety. Turnover was due more to discouragement with the slow progress of the work than to its dangerous nature. Good hard rock miners were difficult to find, since World War I had lured many skilled men to other types of work. The chance to participate in such an heroic project caught the imagination of engineering school students, and many of these young men worked on the drilling, blasting, and mucking crews.

It was vital to get underground before the winter of 1923-24 set in, so excavation was begun without preliminary core drilling to determine the nature of the rock to be encountered. The geologists' estimates proved to be in error. It was thought that a only a few thousand feet of unstable rock existed at the west end. This condition turned out to prevail for almost the entire west half of the bore. While much solid rock was encountered near the east portal, underground water presented another hazard.

Actual construction involved the constant repetition of the cycle of drilling, blasting, mucking (debris removal), enlarging the bore, and setting timbers. Work proceeded around the clock, and a few feet of progress were made on each eight-hour shift. Electric power was used for drilling, for powering the ventilating fans, and for running the narrow gauge trains that brought in supplies and removed muck from the working headings.

SHATTERED ROCK AND UNDERGROUND WATER

The extremely bad rock in the west portal area resulted from tremendous underground pressure. As work advanced, 12x12-inch timbers gave way under the stress. Even the tunnel floor began to buckle and swell upward. Eventually, timbering was replaced by steel supports, but the result was that costs far exceeded the original estimates. An additional $2,500,000 bond issue was sold in March 1925. In contrast, work from the east portal was progressing rapidly through hard rock, the ideal condition for tunneling. Underground water caused some delay, but the apex was passed in November. A third bond issue of $3,500,000 was authorized early the following year.

Then, on February 28, 1926, the most serious water trouble was encountered so suddenly that the men were forced to abandon their machinery and run for their lives. Since work had passed the apex, the tunnel soon filled with water and mud. Huge centrifugal pumps were rushed to the scene, and the water was almost entirely drained. Then a severe blizzard cut power lines leading to East Portal, and the shaft immediately filled again. The flow of water eventually ceased, but the mud hardened, and several thousand feet of the tunnel had to be reexcavated.

The west portal awaits the track laying crew on January 30, 1928, less than a month before the first train. (Moffat Tunnel Commission)

By this time work at the west end almost had been brought to a halt by adverse geologic conditions. Engineers, contractors, and workers were extremely discouraged. George Lewis, a mining engineer with long experience in the Cripple Creek District, had been appointed general manager of the tunnel project. When all other ideas had failed, he conceived the Lewis Traveling Cantilever Girder. This proved to be the salvation of the tunnel project and was the major engineering development to come from it. Essentially, the girder was a device that excavated the top of the tunnel heading and then supported the tunnel roof while the bore was enlarged beneath.

Work was now able to resume at a reasonable pace. However, on the evening of July 30, 1926, a very serious accident occurred. Without warning 125 tons of rock fell from the roof of the railroad tunnel just beyond cross-cut 9 from West Portal. Six men were killed instantly. All work ceased for several days while their bodies were recovered, with the ever present danger that another rock fall could occur at any moment. Twenty-eight men died during the entire construction of the Moffat Tunnel, but this record compares most favorably to that of similar projects in other parts of the world where death tolls ran into the hundreds. The Moffat's safety record has been attributed to careful planning by the contractors and a high level of skill and caution among the workers.

Excavation now progressed at a steady rate and by early 1927 workers at each face of the pioneer bore could hear the blasting at the opposite face. On the morning of February 12, the West Portal graveyard shift, with twenty minutes left of its time, shoved a forty-foot pilot bar through to the opposite facing. The East Portal crew, aware from the sound of what was going on, was ready to grab the bar as it came through, and an excited tug of war ensued. Credit for the victory went to the West Portal gang, and the men were rushed to Denver where they received a welcome usually reserved for returning heroes. Thousands turned out for a parade, and the men spent the night in the Presidential suite of the Cosmopolitan Hotel.

On February 18, 1927, the official holing through ceremonies were held. Dignitaries headed by Colorado Governor William H. Adams and Salt Lake City Mayor Clarence C. Neslen traveled by special train through the usual blizzard over Rollins Pass to West Portal where they were taken about two miles in to cross-cut 13 of the water tunnel. At exactly 8:10 p.m., a series of blasts was set off via telegraph by President Calvin Coolidge from the White House. The sounds of the blasts were transmitted via a national radio hookup and were reported to be heard more clearly in parts of Canada than in Denver.

(Denver Public Library Western History Department)

In the mind of the public the tunnel had been completed, but the main railroad bore still had to be finished. The worst rock of all was encountered at cross-cut 9 of the main tunnel, but it was not what the miners called "fast rock." That is, it did not cave in suddenly, and experienced men developed a sense of knowing when falling particles indicated danger. Three more Lewis girders were placed in service and by June, fifteen faces were being worked simultaneously. Holing through of the railroad tunnel occurred on July 7, 1927, with the West Portal men again the victors. Traditionally, the headings were only a fraction of a inch off. The next day a fourth and final bond issue of $2,750,000 was floated.

All that remained was to complete the track. The entire tunnel, 16 feet wide by 24 feet high, was lined with California Redwood, steel plates, concrete, or gunite (a mixture of sand and concrete shot against the walls and ceiling). Crossties and 110-pound rail began to arrive. Finishing touches were put on both concrete portals, as well as the East Portal snow shed and ventilation housing. Preparations for the opening ceremonies began.

The first freight train passed through the Moffat Tunnel, from west to east on February 24, 1928. It consisted of 12 cars of lumber from the W. H. Wood Lumber and Supply Company of West Portal and took 30 minutes for the passage. Appropriately, Wood had been an associate of David Moffat and had supplied a great quantity of the timber used in the early building of the railroad.

The official opening celebration took place on Sunday, February 26, 1928. Commencing at 8:40 a.m., four special trains left the Moffat Depot on 15th Street in Denver at 15 minute intervals, carrying over 2,500 excursionists. Dignitaries included Governor Adams, ex-Governor Shoup, Denver Mayor Benjamin Stapleton, former Mayor Dewey C. Bailey, Major John F. Bowman of Salt Lake City, President Robinson of the Tunnel Commission and President W. R. Freeman of the Denver & Salt Lake Railway. The trains arrived at East Portal starting about noon. The invocation and speeches were broadcast by radio station KOA and transmitted nationwide. A gold spike was provided by the *Denver Post* which, in its style of the day, claimed credit for just about the entire project. A time capsule was sealed which contained among other items the 2,500 ticket stubs of the first passengers. Strangely, this was stored and forgotten in the Moffat's Denver station and was not actually placed in the tunnel portal until 1947. The two governors, after 15 strikes and ten misses, managed to drive the last spike and at exactly 2:01 p.m., locomotive 205, a veteran of many winters on Rollins Pass, entered the tunnel. Engineer Louis A. Larsen, who had been with the Moffat Road from its inception, was at the throttle.

A popular expression developed among Moffat Road old timers—whether employee, passenger, or shipper—that the tunnel had taken "23 miles off the route and 23 days off the schedule." Except in a few instances, this was somewhat of an exaggeration, but the comparative statistics of the new line compared with those of the old hill route are significant. Indeed, 23 miles were eliminated. The maximum grade was halved from four to two percent, and the maximum elevation was reduced by 2,440 feet. Train lengths could be doubled, but most important was the elimination of the tremendous cost, in both dollars and human effort, required to keep the old line open during the long and severe winters.

THE MOFFAT TUNNEL COMPARED WITH OTHER MAJOR RAILROAD TUNNELS OF THE WORLD AT THE TIME IT WAS COMPLETED

Name	Construction Period	Length In Miles	Boring Months	Average Daily Progress (Feet)	Completion Cost	Location
Mt. Cenis	1857-1870	7.97	157	4.4	$15,000,000	France - Italy
Hoosac	1858-1874	4.75	241	3.0	10,000,000	Massachusetts
St. Gotthard	1872-1882	9.26	88	6.2	11,300,000	Switzerland - France - Italy
Arlberg	1880-1883	6.20	40	13.6	5,900,000	Austria - France
Simplon	1898-1905	12.40	78	13.7	15,700,000	Switzerland - Italy
Loetschberg	1906-1911	9.30	54	14.2	10,300,000	Switzerland
Connaught	1913-1916	5.02	22	21.1	6,000,000	British Columbia
Moffat	1923-1927	6.21	48	21.0	15,600,000	Colorado
Cascade	1926-1929	7.79	37	36.9	15,000,000	Washington

(Edward T. Bollinger and Frederick Bauer, *The Moffat Road*)

The Burlington's original Zephyr 9900 enters the Moffat Tunnel enroute to the opening of the Dotsero Cutoff on June 16, 1934. The photographer superimposed more dramatic mountain scenery than actually exists at this loca-

THE DOTSERO CUTOFF

Completion of the tunnel, however, was not the last step in the fulfillment of David Moffat's dream. The Denver & Salt Lake Railway remained a short line ending at Craig, Colorado, 231 miles northwest of Denver. Even before the tunnel had been finished, the owners of the railroad, still under the able leadership of Gerald Hughes, were planning to extend the track to Salt Lake City, either along the originally surveyed route through the Uintah Basin of Utah or by construction of the 40-mile cutoff to the Denver & Rio Grande Western main line at Dotsero, east of Glenwood Canyon. This plan was soon thought of as the more practical one, and a separate company, the Denver & Salt Lake Western, was incorporated for its construction.

At that time in its history, Rio Grande was controlled jointly by the Missouri Pacific and Western Pacific railroads. While WP was in favor of the cutoff, as it would offer a connection to the east via Chicago Burlington & Quincy 175 miles shorter than the old route via Pueblo, there was obviously no advantage in the plan for either Rio Grande or Missouri Pacific. Thus the managements of these railroads resisted all efforts to enlist

their support in building the Dotsero line. The Interstate Commerce Commission, whose approval had to be gained in order for construction to begin, required that one of the transcontinental railroads build and operate the route, since the tiny and financially weak D&SL would be unable to run it profitably. When the Burlington appeared ready to buy the Moffat Road and build the cutoff, Rio Grande at last realized that completion of the project was inevitable and drew up its own proposal. At the same time, it proceeded to buy a majority interest in the D&SL.

This was approved by the ICC, and construction began in November 1932 with funds provided by a Reconstruction Finance Corporation loan. Although the route was only 38 miles in length through relatively easy country, work proceeded at a glacial pace. Rio Grande still seemed to be delaying the opening of the new line as long as possible. Finally, on June 16, 1934, the last spike was driven, and the opening celebration was held at the new town of Bond, on the eastern end of the cutoff. After 67 long years of struggle, David Moffat's ambition had been realized, and Denver was on a transcontinental route.

A great deal of work still had to be done in order to bring the Moffat route up to main line standards after years of operation on extremely limited funds. All during the remainder of the 1930s heavy rail and ballast were laid, wooden trestles were replaced by steel bridges or fills, and curvature was reduced. The Moffat Tunnel itself was lined with either concrete or gunite for most of its length in 1937, and welded rail was laid throughout. By the summer of 1939, the rebuilding program was almost complete and D&RGW's heaviest motive power could operate over the line. On June 11th, a new luxury passenger train, the *Exposition Flyer* made its first run through the Rockies from Chicago to San Francisco via the Burlington and Western Pacific connections.

The Moffat Tunnel met its greatest test during the 1941-45 war years with as many as 30 freight, passenger, and troop trains passing through in a single day. Its importance was emphasized in late 1943 when the route was closed for ten weeks by a disastrous fire in Tunnel 10 west of Plainview. If the line had not been reopened by the end of the year, a traffic blockage would have resulted, since alternate routes would have been unable to absorb the additional burden as wartime traffic continued to grow.

On April 11, 1947, Denver & Salt Lake was merged with D&RGW, which came out of receivership on the same day. The continued prosperity of the Moffat Tunnel route was symbolized two years later when the *California Zephyr* replaced the old *Exposition Flyer* as the premier train on the CB&Q/D&RGW/WP Chicago-to-California route. The *CZ* included through New York-Oakland sleeping cars, and the train soon became one of the most popular in the United States.

In retrospect, it is probable that if Denver had never been on a direct transcontinental railroad line, the city would still have achieved its present importance and prosperity. It grew and thrived for many years before the Moffat Tunnel was completed, and today the existence of the tunnel is not the most vital factor in the economy of either Denver or the western slope of the state. However, the availability of an efficient rail system to transport its natural resources and to bring in goods from other parts of the country has benefitted a vast area of Colorado. A large part of this lies outside the Moffat Tunnel Improvement District and thus gave no financial support to the project.

Able management by the tunnel commissioners elected over the years allowed the discontinuance of all tax levies within the district as of December 31, 1971, well in advance of the June 15, 1983, retirement date of the last bonds. Actual construction cost came to approximately $18 million, or about three million dollars per mile. The cost of financing the bond issue over a 50 year period brought the total to about $44 million. Even with an allowance for a half century of inflation, this compares most favorably with the $117 million in construction cost alone of just the initial 1.7 mile bore of the Eisenhower Tunnel completed in 1972 on Interstate Highway 70.

On September 24, 1979, the American Society of Civil Engineers designated the Moffat Tunnel as a National Historic Civil Engineering Landmark.

After the final bond payment of $266,000 to the Irving Trust Company in New York on December 17, 1982, there appeared to be no further purpose for the tun-

The crew of this Moffat Road steam shovel stops work for a few minutes to pose for the photographer. The large excavating machine is working on a cut for the new Dotsero Cutoff.
(Robert Jensen collection)

nel commission. At D&RGW's prodding, State Senator Meiklejohn and Representative Mielk introduced Senate Bill No. 87, an act for the dissolution of the Moffat Tunnel District. However, the bill was allowed to die in committee.

Meanwhile, the railroad had spent about one million dollars to revise the ventilation system. Locomotive exhaust now goes eastward, the natural air flow direction, instead of out the west portal. This change also benefitted the Winter Park ski slopes. New fans, blowers, and electrical system at East Portal have improved the tunnel environment for train crews.

The last *Rio Grande Zephyr* passed through the tunnel on April 24, 1983. Amtrak's *California Zephyr* was to have begun service over the Moffat line the next day, but a tremendous mudslide and its resulting lake at Thistle, Utah, had closed the railroad until July 16. For almost two months, through traffic had to detour over Union Pacific through Wyoming. The reverse situation had occurred in January 1949 when Overland Route trains were routed through the Moffat while UP dug out from a severe blizzard.

In 1983, the railroad picture in the West began to change dramatically. Denver businessman Philip Anschutz purchased D&RGW outright and, five years later, acquired the ailing Southern Pacific. He promptly merged the two western rail icons. Then in 1996, SP was acquired by Union Pacific. It is ironic that, a century after UP's E. H. Harriman had attempted to defeat him, David Moffat's railroad now belongs to his old corporate enemy.

Change was also in the wind for the Moffat Tunnel Commission. In 1996, the Colorado legislature passed a bill to terminate the commission altogether. First, the railroad and water tunnels had to be sold. In January 1998, the Denver Water Board purchased the latter for seven million dollars, but Union Pacific's offer for the railroad bore was deemed inadequate. UP continues to pay a bargain rent of only $12,000 annually. The Moffat Tunnel Improvement District was dissolved on February 1, 1998, when the tunnel and other remaining assets were transferred to the Colorado Department of Local Affairs.

The Moffat Tunnel is destined for the foreseeable future to provide a transportation artery for two commodities vital to Colorado and the West—coal and water. Several daily trains transport up to 12,000 tons of coal each from the vast deposits of northwestern Colorado to the major cities on the eastern slope as well as to other parts of the United States. Other trains carry transcontinental merchandise and commodities to and from the West Coast. The *California Zephyr* traverses the Moffat during its Chicago - San Francisco Bay area journey, as does the seasonal Winter Park *Ski Train* and an occasional *American Orient Express*.

Water first flowed eastward through the pioneer bore under the Continental Divide on June 10, 1936, and today this is a major source of supply for Denver's ever-growing metropolitan population. Thus the tunnel will continue to be of value to Colorado for reasons perhaps undreamed of by David Moffat.

An unidentified Moffat Road 2-8-0 pushes an inspection train through the eastern part of the tunnel, prior to the installation of concrete lining. (Denver Pubic Library Western History Department)

We own and offer for prompt delivery

Moffat Tunnel Bonds

To Yield Five Per Cent

District includes City of Denver. Bonds payable from ad valorem taxes. Exempt from Federal Income Tax and Colorado Property Taxes.

Place your orders with us

Bosworth Chanute & Co

INVESTMENT SECURITIES - 17TH & CALIFORNIA

Main 1874

This September 10, 1923, newspaper advertisement is typical of many that were placed by Denver investment brokers. All four bond issues sold out quickly. (Moffat Tunnel Commission)

Western Slope water flows from the east portal of the pioneer bore immediately south of the railroad tunnel. (Kenton Forrest photo)

SOURCES AND BIBLIOGRAPHY

Athearn, Robert G., *Rebel of the Rockies*, Yale University Press, New Haven, 1962 (published in paperback under the title *The Denver & Rio Grande Western Railroad*, University of Nebraska Press, 1977).

Bollinger, Edward T. *Rails That Climb*, The Rydal Press, Santa Fe, 1950; revised edition, Colorado Railroad Museum, Golden, 1979.

Bollinger, Edward T. and Frederick Bauer, *The Moffat Road*, Sage Books, Denver, 1962.

Boner, Harold, *The Giant's Ladder*, Kalmbach Publishing Co., Milwaukee, 1962.

McMechen, Edgar Carlisle, *The Moffat Tunnel of Colorado*, Wahlgreen Publishing Co., Denver, 1927.

Thode, Jackson, C., *A Century of Passenger Trains...And Then Some...*, Rocky Mountain Railroad Club, Denver, 2001.

Various newspapers, scrapbooks, timetables, folders, and maps in the files of the Moffat Tunnel Commission; the Robert W. Richardson Library at Colorado Railroad Museum, and the Western History Department of the Denver Public Library.

EAST PORTAL

These two pages illustrate the early stages of construction at East Portal during 1922-1924. At the top left is a general view of the area from the first level of the old route over Rollins Pass. The two survey lines in the center of the picture point upward to the 13,250-foot summit of James Peak and down to the tunnel portal, while the railroad grade from Tolland approaches from the left. Directly left is a closer view of the construction camp, showing the long trestle where the narrow gauge mine cars dumped the muck removed from the tunnel. The resulting fill is seen at the bottom, while *(below)* a small ditcher works in the cut leading to the railroad tunnel. (all, Moffat Tunnel Commission)

(above) Work progresses at the railroad tunnel. Today, this area is covered by a long concrete snowshed directly behind the portal itself. Small mine cars from the tunnel transferred their loads to four-cubic-yard capacity cars that took the debris out on the fill trestle. To the right is one of the steam dinkeys used until electric trolley locomotives arrived. (below) No. 3E, the *David H. Moffat*, poses with a loaded train of four-yard cars. (all, Moffat Tunnel Commission)

(left) Forms are set for pouring the concrete snowshed. (below) The east portal housing itself takes shape in October 1927. (both, Moffat Tunnel Commission)

(above) Denver & Salt Lake 4-6-0 No. 303 saw use as a source of steam power during the final stages of construction. (Denver Public Library Western History Department) The contemporary view below clearly illustrates the air intake dampers and the canvas door that is lowered when the ventilation fans are in use. This system obviated the need to electrify the railroad through the tunnel, thereby avoiding additional expense and operating problems. (Kenton Forrest photo)

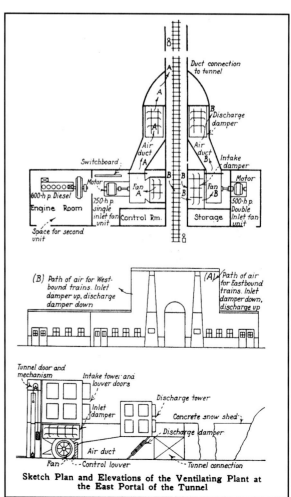

Sketch Plan and Elevations of the Ventilating Plant at the East Portal of the Tunnel

TUNNEL BUILDERS

Many people with many different skills were required for the successful completion of this massive project. Above is the timekeeper's office at West Portal and the clerks responsible for keeping accurate pay records. *(below)* Mess halls at both portals were open around the clock. An abundance of good food was a necessity in maintaining high morale among the workers. *(lower right)* This kitchen crew looks quite capable of handling any crowd. At the right center, copied from an old news-paper clipping, is a picture of little Thelma Wagner, the first new citizen of East Portal. (all, Moffat Tunnel Commission)

First Baby Born at East Portal, Thelma Wagner, Whose Daddy Is One of the Workmen

The two photographs at the left illustrate the excavation process. The timber roof arch with cordwood and dry packing is placed, then the bore is widened below. Cross cut No.3 switch from the water tunnel to the main bore is at the bottom left, while at the lower right is the ideal solid rock for tunneling that existed for only a short distance near the east portal. Work progresses *(below center)* at the west portal before construction of the concrete portal itself. (all, Moffat Tunnel Commission)

The Lewis Traveling Cantilever Girder saved the tunnel project from failure. At the top left, Assistant Superintendent P. L. Hamilton, C. C. Tinkler, and Superintendent William Fowler inspect the cantilever needle bar. Above, General Manager George Lewis and C. C. Tinkler with the Osgood Compressed Air Shovel that mucked out the debris as the Lewis Girder supported the roof. *(left)* The Osgood shovel loads one of the muck cars. Below is a diagram of the girder from a contemporary issue of *Railway Age*. (all, Moffat Tunnel Commission)

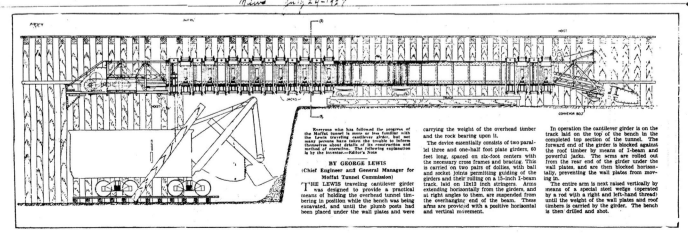

THIS DEVICE TURNED DEFEAT INTO VICTORY ON TUNNEL JOB

Everyone who has followed the progress of the Moffat tunnel is more or less familiar with the Lewis traveling cantilever girder, but not many persons have taken the trouble to inform themselves about details of its construction and method of operation. The following explanation is by the inventor.—*Editor's Note*

BY GEORGE LEWIS
(Chief Engineer and General Manager for Moffat Tunnel Commission)

THE LEWIS traveling cantilever girder was designed to provide a practical means of holding the overhead tunnel timbering in position while the bench was being excavated, and until the plumb posts had been placed under the wall plates and were carrying the weight of the overhead timber and the rock bearing upon it.

The device essentially consists of two parallel three and one-half foot plate girders, 60 feet long, spaced on six-foot centers with the necessary cross frames and bracing. This is carried on two pairs of dollies, with ball and socket joints permitting guiding of the girders and their rolling on a 15-inch I-beam track, laid on 12x12 inch stringers. Arms extending horizontally from the girders, and at right angles to them, are suspended from the overhanging end of the beam. These arms are provided with a positive horizontal and vertical movement.

In operation the cantilever girder is on the track laid on the top of the bench in the completed top section of the tunnel. The forward end of the girder is blocked against the roof timber by means of I-beam and powerful jacks. The arms are rolled out from the rear end of the girder under the wall plates, and are then blocked horizontally, preventing the wall plates from moving in.

The entire arm is next raised vertically by means of a special steel wedge (operated by a rod with a right and left-hand thread) until the weight of the wall plates and roof timbers is carried by the girder. The bench is then drilled and shot.

East Portal
MOFFAT TUNNEL
Celebration July 4th
Given by East Portal Athletic Club

BIG SMOKER
Boxing, Wrestling and Blanket Wrestling
3:00 P. M.
Admission $1.00 Plus War Tax   Ladies Free

FREE   PICTURE SHOW   FREE

BIG FIREWORKS
Free   8:30 P. M.   Free

9:00 P.M. Hard Time Dance 9:00 P.M.
Harmony Peerless Orchestra of Denver
Prize for Best Costume
Admission $1.00 Plus War Tax   Ladies Free
Refreshments Free

Frequent social gatherings were organized by various groups at the two construction camps. A poster for the July 4, 1926, celebration at East Portal is reproduced at the left. The group gathered below on October 8, 1925, includes many individuals who played important roles in the Moffat Tunnel project. From left, in the front row are Charles H. Wheeler, L. D. Blauvelt, J. Vipond Davies, David W. Brunton, J. Waldo Smith, W. N. W. Blayney, and West Portal Resident Engineer A. A. Kauffman. In the back are General Manager George Lewis, Charles H. Leckenby, William P. Robinson, Charles MacAllister Willcox, F. C. Hitchcock, Mr. Hamilton, C. C. Tinkler, A. H. Baer, Mr. Rhodes, and Resident Engineer James Cohig. Wheeler, Blayney, Leckenby, Robinson, and Wilcox were tunnel commissioners; Blauvelt, Davis, Brunton, and Smith were consulting engineers, Hitchcock and Tinkler were the contractors. (all, Moffat Tunnel Commission)

The East Portal construction camp is seen at the left, with the various buildings used by the contractor and as living quarters for the workers.

(left) Tunnel engineers McGrury and Paterson are seen on a raft in the water tunnel on March 1, 1926, the day after East Portal crews encountered the most serious flow of underground water from Crater Lake. Work was delayed for three months while the tunnel was drained and re-excavated. *(below)* Rescue work proceeds at crosscut 9E, West Portal, on July 31, 1926, after the cave-in that killed six men. In the center foreground are George Lewis and F. C. Hitchcock who personally supervised the effort.

Moffat Road 4-4-0 No. 390 and ditcher 10104 are shown working at East Portal in October 1924. Perhaps as the 390 simmered in the high Rocky Mountain air, she thought of her youth as a fast passenger engine far away and long ago on the Chesapeake Beach Railway, an ill-fated project of David Moffat and Otto Mears in Washington, D.C. (all, Moffat Tunnel Commission)

WEST PORTAL

(top left) At the beginning of construction at West Portal, a ponderous ditcher is eased across the Fraser River on a rather perilous looking bridge. In the center of the page is seen Wood's sawmill at Irving's Spur (now Winter Park). This mill shipped the first freight through the Moffat Tunnel in 1928. At the left is a view of the Osgood Compressed Air Shovel in action at the west portal of the railroad tunnel in early 1924. (center, Denver Public Library Western History Department; others, Moffat Tunnel Commission.)

The "Drill Doctor" performed the vital task of sharpening thousands of drill bits needed in the hard rock drilling from the East Portal end. (above, Moffat Tunnel Commission)

At the top of the page, the bents are in place for the West Portal dump trestle. The trestle was in use by January 1924 *(left)* and the timber framing shed, where the supports used in tunnel construction were fabricated, is also shown. At the bottom is a general view of the area as it appeared the following year. The mountain slope above the newly completed railroad grade is the site of today's Winter Park ski slope. (all, Moffat Tunnel Commission)

The tunnel contractors used an interesting combination of animal and mechanical power. Teams of horses hauled in the undercarriage of one of the electric mine locomotives *(top left)* and one of the Lewis Traveling Cantilever Girders *(left)*, while a chain drive, hard tire dump truck works at West Portal *(above)*. Below is a view of the West Portal camp as seen from the top of what is today's ski slope. The railroad tunnel portal is visible in the lower right corner of the photograph. (all, Moffat Tunnel Commission)

By early May 1927, the framing work for the concrete portal itself was in place *(right)* and after the concrete had been poured, sample lettering was applied.

This view looks outward from within the west portal on a frigid day. Workers emerging from the tunnel were required to take hot and cold showers in order to cool off gradually prior to encountering the icy winter air. (all, Moffat Tunnel Commission)

LAST BARRIER IS HOLED THRU

Moffat-Evans Tunnel Links East and West After Four-Year-Task; Trains Soon to Go Under James Peak

The railroad bore of the Moffat-Evans tunnel was holed thru Thursday afternoon.

When daylight showed thru the big bore and a draft of air swept from the west to the east side, Colorado had realized a dream of years.

The backbone of the continental divide had been broken and the tunnel digging venture, which began in September, 1923, had been crowned with success.

The year 1927 was one of fulfillment for all who were involved with the building of the tunnel. Above is the victorious crew who holed through the pioneer bore on February 12, about to depart for the celebration that awaited them in Denver. At the right, George Lewis, the man who saved the project from failure, poses under a section of newly completed concrete lining. For a short time, the Denver newspapers referred to the "Moffat-Evans Tunnel," as illustrated by the July 7,1927, *Denver Post* headline at the top of the page. (all, Moffat Tunnel Commission)

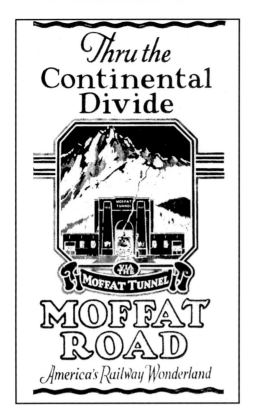

On an unrecorded date in the summer of 1927 and without fanfare, Denver & Salt Lake Railway 120 was the first locomotive to enter Moffat Tunnel. (Denver Public Library Western History Department) Two of the famed Moffat mallets, Nos. 207 and 200, blast through Tolland with 13 cars of the third special train enroute to the opening ceremony on February 26, 1928. One would like to think that the spirit of David Moffat was aboard the *Marcia* as it waited its turn to pass through the tunnel at the end of one of the opening day specials *(below)*. Today, this private car of the famous railroad builder is displayed in Craig, Colorado, the end of the line for the Moffat Road. (both photos, Otto C. Perry, Denver Public Library Western History Department OP-11272 and OP-11396)

OPENING DAY
FEB. 26, 1928

The program reproduced here is from an original in the collection of Elmer Schlotz, who was one of the 2,500 passengers on the first trains. This order *(right)* was issued for the first train through the Moffat Tunnel. Engine 205, with engineer Louis Larsen at the throttle, led the train from East Portal through the tunnel, then turned at Irvings for the return to Denver. The train order was issued by longtime Moffat Dispatcher J. B. Culbertson. (Mrs. Louis A. Larsen collection)

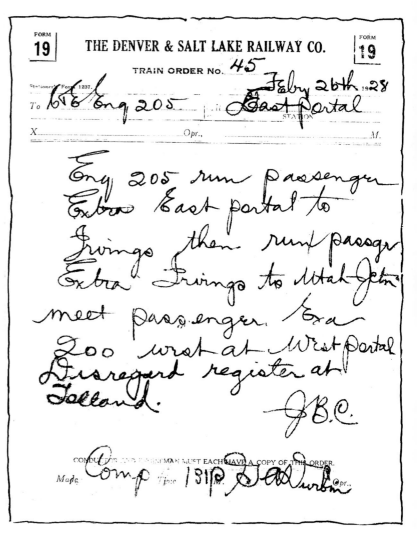

PROGRAM
Ceremonies at Opening of the Moffat Tunnel

FEBRUARY 26, 1928 -- EAST PORTAL, COLO.

12:15 P. M.—Invocation by The Reverend Charles Marshall.
12:16 P. M.—Driving of the Gold Spike by ex-Governor Oliver H. Shoup and Governor William H. Adams.
12:17 P. M.—Formal delivery of possession of Railroad Tunnel to The Denver & Salt Lake Railway Company, by William P. Robinson, President of the Moffat Tunnel Commission.
12:20 P. M.—Acceptance of Tunnel on behalf of The Denver & Salt Lake Railway Company, by William R. Freeman, President.
12:21 P. M.—Address by Honorable Oliver H. Shoup, ex-Governor of Colorado.
12:24 P. M.—Address by Honorable William H. Adams, Governor of Colorado.
12:27 P. M.—Address by Honorable Dewey C. Bailey, ex-Mayor of Denver.
12:30 P. M.—Address by Honorable John F. Bowman, Mayor of Salt Lake City.
12:33 P. M.—Address by Honorable Benjamin F. Stapleton, Mayor of Denver.
 1:20 P. M.—First train enters Tunnel.

Time Table for First Passenger Train Through the Moffat Tunnel

Going	Elevation	Station	Miles	Returning
8:40 a.m.	5,170	Lv........DENVER	0	5:15 p.m.
8:54 a.m.	5,215	Lv........UTAH JUNCTION............	3	5:02 p.m.
9:04 a.m.	5,268	Lv........RALSTON	7	4:55 p.m.
9:18 a.m.	5,687	Lv........LEYDEN JUNCTION........	13	4:42 p.m.
9:30 a.m.	6,162	Lv........ARENA	18	4:30 p.m.
9:55 a.m.	6,783	Lv........PLAINVIEW	25	4:16 p.m.
10:20 a.m.	7,457	Lv........CRESCENT	32	3:55 p.m.
10:45 a.m.	7,958	Lv.......PINECLIFF	37	3:40 p.m.
11:00 a.m.	8,367	Lv........ROLLINSVILLE	42	3:27 p.m.
11:20 a.m.	8,889	Lv........TOLLAND	47	3:15 p.m.
11:40 a.m.	9,198	Ar........EAST PORTAL...........	50	3:00 p.m.
1:20 p.m.	9,198	Lv........EAST PORTAL...........	50	3:00 p.m.
1:40 p.m.	9,085	Ar........WEST PORTAL...........	56	2:40 p.m.

Fortunately for the celebrants, the opening day offered sunny skies and dry ground at East Portal, where the Society of Colorado Pioneers *(above)* posed en masse. (Denver Public Library Western History Department) Standing in front of D&SL 205, the crew members of the first train have their photo taken along with several of the passengers. Below, many participants had a long walk from the four specials to the portal for the ceremonies. (both, CRRM collection)

All Ready for 'Long Sleep'

THIS VAULT CONTAINS HISTORICAL DATA CONCERNING MOFFAT TUNNEL TO BE OPENED FEBRUARY 26, 1978

PEOPLE in 1978 will read about how The NEWSpapers of 1928 told of one of Colorado's most notable achievements, completion of the Moffat tunnel. The edition of The Rocky Mountain News, shown above being held by Miss Violet Shaeffer, is one that will be buried in a steel vault to be placed in the tunnel. The vault above will be opened in 1978. Stubs of tickets held by the 2,590 passengers to make the trip, also will be placed in the vault.

Colorado Governor Adams and ex-Governor Shoup listen to one of the speeches. Then the governor hammers in the last spike as a newspaper photographer records the historic moment. The entire ceremony was broadcast over KOA radio. Below are the large bronze plaques which bracket the portal. (all, Denver Public Library Western History Department)

With a newsreel camera and crew perched in front of its smoke box, No. 205 was the center of attention. At 2:01 p.m. it steamed into the tunnel with the first official train. Union Pacific, an old enemy of the Moffat, supplied a good portion of the rolling stock used on this day. (all, Denver Public Library Western History Department; Otto Perry photo OP-11395 at bottom)

No. 200 emerges at West Portal in a view that enjoyed wide circulation in a color post card. (Denver Public Library Western History Department) In the summer of 1940, the railroad installed high pressure water nozzles at both portals to wash soot and cinders from car windows. This was done only when the temperature was above freezing. The drawing below is of a revised system to accommodate the new *California Zephyr* vista-dome cars. The change was never made because diesel locomotives had eliminated the problem. (CRRM collection)

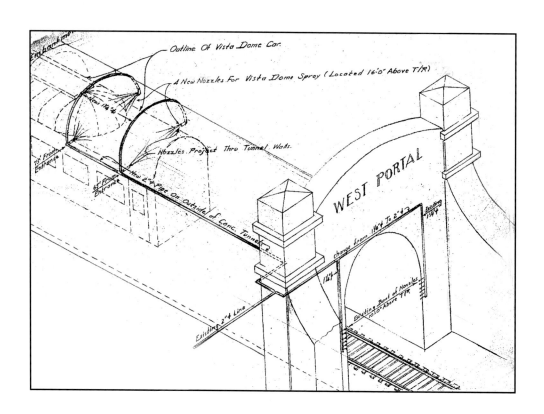

Moffat mallet 212 eases a steel form into the west portal during the concrete lining of the tunnel in 1933 by the Blaw-Knox Company of Pittsburgh, Pennsylvania. The man on the running board leaning on the front of the cab is Robert S. Mayo who supervised the job for the contractor and had previously worked for Hitchcock & Tinkler during the original tunnel construction. (Blaw-Knox photo, Robert S. Mayo collection) Below is a view of the West Portal box car station with No. 205, which had starred on opening day, as rear end helper on a Denver-bound freight. In 1939, this area became the base of the Winter Park ski slopes. (CRRM collection)

Otto Perry took many photos of early operation through the tunnel. At the top, Denver & Salt Lake 301 rolls train No.1 through West Portal in December 1933, when the tunnel still served just as a short route to Craig. Above, No. 300 performs the same duty in March 1935. By this time, however, the Dotsero Cutoff had been open for several months and D&RGW 1200 approaches West Portal *(below)* with train 6, the *Panoramic*, enroute from Salt Lake City to Denver. These Mikados and the 3400 series 2-8-8-2s were the heaviest Rio Grande power that could operate over the Moffat Line until the late 1930s. (Otto C. Perry photos OP-11309, OP-11299, OP-10155 - Denver Public Library Western History Department)

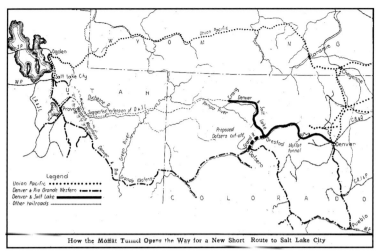

How the Moffat Tunnel Opens the Way for a New Short Route to Salt Lake City

(Moffat Tunnel Commission)

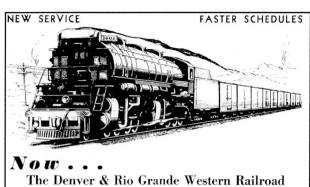

NEW SERVICE   FASTER SCHEDULES

Now . . .
The Denver & Rio Grande Western Railroad
offers
FAST, DEPENDABLE FREIGHT SERVICE
Via **TWO** Routes
between **Colorado, Utah and the Pacific Coast**

A New and Shorter Route	An Established Fast Route
via	*via*
Denver, the Moffat Tunnel and the Dotsero Cut-off	Colorado Springs, Pueblo and the Royal Gorge

THROUGH MANIFEST FREIGHT TRAINS VIA BOTH ROUTES ARE COORDINATED WITH THOSE OF CONNECTING LINES, INSURING PROMPT INTERCHANGE AND DEPENDABLE MOVEMENT OF CARLOAD AND LESS THAN CARLOAD SHIPMENTS

For further information, ask any Traffic Representative listed on pages 53 and 54
ROUTE YOUR FREIGHT
via
THE DENVER & RIO GRANDE WESTERN RAILROAD
GEORGE WILLIAMS, Freight Traffic Manager, Denver, Colo.

THE DOTSERO CUTOFF

(above right) This advertisement appeared in the Rio Grande's Summer 1934 passenger timetable. (CRRM collection) Immaculately groomed D&RGW Nos. 1177 and 802 lead the 12-car third section of the special train out of Denver for the opening of the cutoff on June 16, 1934. (Otto C. Perry, Denver Public Library Western History Department OP-10142) Burlington Zephyr 9900 pokes its nose out of the tunnel on the same day. This first diesel powered, stainless steel train had completed its non-stop Denver-Chicago run just three weeks earlier and was one of the world's most famous trains. The photographer was unhappy with the local topography and borrowed a portion of Gore Canon to give a more dramatic background to the scene. (Burlington Northern)

THE MOFFAT ROUTE

(left) West Portal Agent Lambert Howell stands at the grimy tunnel entrance on a winter afternoon in 1936. The large wooden doors were found to serve no useful purpose and were shortly removed. Notice the accumulation of cinders between the rails that had to be removed by section crews in their spare time. Combined with moisture, the cinders formed sulphuric acid, greatly cutting the life of the rails which had to be replaced in 1938, 1943, 1951, and 1961. Diesel locomotives eventually eliminated the problem. Below, No. 303 enters the black hole of the Moffat in November 1934.(A. Wass photo, CRRM collection) Although Rio Grande operated over the Moffat Road for 13 years prior to merger, it was extremely rare to see locomotives of the two railroads on the same train. D&RGW 804 and D&SL 402 doublehead one of the first ski trains (then called snow trains) to Hot Sulphur Springs on February 9, 1936. (Otto C. Perry photo, Denver Public Library Western History Department OP-10076)

Above, No. 3405, a compound 2-8-8-2 equipped with a smoke deflector, auxiliary tender, and gas masks, enters the east portal at five miles-per-hour. The life of the crew under such conditions can only be imagined. *(right)* Train 2 enters the Moffat, as seen from the rear vestibule. On another occasion, it emerges at East Portal on a warm afternoon in June 1941. (Otto C. Perry, Denver Public Library Western History Department OP-10639, OP-11227, OP-11254)

The Moffat mallets were involved in several runaways during the years of operation over Rollins Pass, and after the opening of the tunnel, No. 215 took one more fling. While switching at East Portal on November 5, 1935, 39 loaded coal cars got away from her, and she was running in excess of 60 MPH before overturning near Rollinsville. Engineer Ohrns was injured as he jumped from the cab. A D&RGW wrecker had plenty of work to do the next day, but No. 215 survived to become Rio Grande 3374 after the 1947 merger. (Otto C. Perry, Denver Public Library Western History Department OP-11390, OP-11391)

On a happier day, D&RGW 4-8-4 No. 1702 heads the eastbound *Exposition Flyer* on the two percent descending grade near Tolland, November 16, 1941. This train was the predecessor of the *California Zephyr* on the Chicago-San Francisco run. The snowy summit just over the locomotive stack is James Peak, beneath which the Moffat Tunnel passes. (Richard H. Kindig)

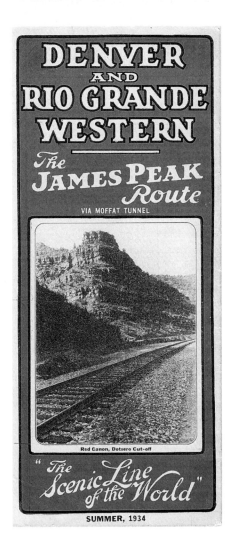

During the first two years after the opening of the Dotsero Cutoff, the new line was promoted as "The James Peak Route" with the tunnel getting only incidental notice; thereafter, the tunnel itself got star billing in all promotional literature. (two timetable covers, CRRM collection) Rio Grande's 3400 series mallets became as familiar on the Moffat Route as the D&SL's own 200s. Below, No. 3403 leads the *Ute*, a fast freight, through Winter Park, which had been renamed from West Portal on December 1, 1939. Rio Grande was a pioneer in offering piggyback service, as evidenced by the second car in the train. (Otto C. Perry photo, Denver Public Library Western History Department OP-10632)

By 1939, rebuilding of the Moffat Road had reached the point where even Rio Grande's mighty 3600 class 2-8-8-2s could be operated. The 3616 emerges at Winter Park with a remarkably clean stack. Ultimately, the ventilation problem in the tunnel was solved by the diesel electric locomotive, Rio Grande being one of the first railroads to order the new 5400-horsepower units from the Electro-Motive Division of General Motors. No. 541 is seen below at Plainview on its first trip westward, April 5, 1942. (Otto C. Perry photos OP-10765, OP-10832, Denver Pubic Library Western History Department)

In March 1946, only a year before the end of the Denver & Salt Lake as a separate corporation, 2-8-2 No. 408 and 2-6-6-0 No. 201 depart from East Portal with a 47-car freight. The tunnel survey lines are still clearly visible on the mountain in the background. (Richard H. Kindig photo)

On August 15, 1948, Otto Perry took these three photographs at East Portal that represent a transition of eras for the Moffat Tunnel. At the top, D&RGW 1035 (nee D&SL 119) arrives with the Craig train, which faithfully provided passenger service to northwestern Colorado for over 60 years. The 3600s would see a few more years of use, as depicted by the 3606 leaving the tunnel with a 62-car freight at 10 MPH. Shortly, the westbound *Exposition Flyer* arrived behind a shiny set of Alco passenger units. Notice the interesting consist of ex-troop sleeper baggage car, heavyweight Pullmans, and vista-domes intended for the *California Zephyr* a few months hence. Otto's 1935 Ford is visible just to the left of the locomotive. (Denver Public Library Western History Department OP-10106, OP-10716, OP-10868)

In early 1949, Union Pacific's mainline across Wyoming was blocked by a severe prairie blizzard, with a large portion of Overland Route traffic being diverted via the Moffat Tunnel Route. The eastbound streamlined *City of Portland* is seen at Plainview with 15 cars trailing its four F3 units.(Richard H. Kindig) At the left, D&RGW 3618 and 1705 pause at East Portal on July 23, 1950, during a Rocky Mountain Railroad Club 500-mile steam-powered excursion over both the Moffat Tunnel and Royal Gorge Routes. A ticket on the 16-car special cost just ten dollars. *(below)* Otto Perry ventured onto the Winter Park ski slope one winter morning in 1953 to get this fine view of the *California Zephyr* drifting out of the west portal behind Alco units 6011-6012-6013. (lower two photos, Otto C. Perry, Denver Public Library Western History Department OP-10776, OP-10998)

An era ends on October 27, 1956, as the last two steam locomotives to operate through the tunnel, 2-8-8-2s 3609 and 3619, wait at Tolland for a westbound diesel freight to pass. Two years later *(center)*, the *Prospector*, with four heavyweight Pullmans in its usually streamlined consist, approaches East Portal on the first leg of its overnight journey to Salt Lake City. (Otto C. Perry photos, Denver Public Library Western History Department OP-10731, OP-10888) At the bottom of the page, the *Ski Train* pulls into Winter Park to load for the return trip to Denver on a snowy winter afternoon in the early 1970s. (CRRM collection)

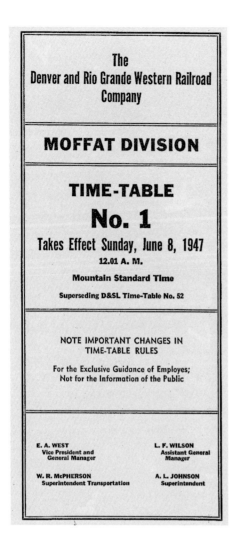

The
Denver and Rio Grande Western Railroad
Company

MOFFAT DIVISION

TIME-TABLE
No. 1
Takes Effect Sunday, June 8, 1947
12.01 A. M.
Mountain Standard Time
Superseding D&SL Time-Table No. 52

NOTE IMPORTANT CHANGES IN
TIME-TABLE RULES

For the Exclusive Guidance of Employes;
Not for the Information of the Public

E. A. WEST
Vice President and
General Manager

L. F. WILSON
Assistant General
Manager

W. R. McPHERSON
Superintendent Transportation

A. L. JOHNSON
Superintendent

One day in the early 1960s, the *Yampa Valley Mail* had an extra coach and the lounge car *Glenwood Canon* added to its usual consist so that Alco PA 6001 required the help of GP9 No. 5952. Visible just over the last car is a portion of the old four percent grade of the Rollins Pass line. (Otto C. Perry photo, Denver Public Library Western History Department OP-10969; timetable and operating rules, CRRM collection)

6-F. TRAIN OPERATION THROUGH MOFFAT TUNNEL.

Not more than one train will be permitted to occupy track in Moffat Tunnel between the east siding switch at Winter Park and the crossover switch at East Portal (either on siding or main track, according to how the west siding switch at East Portal may be lined) except that a helper engine may be uncoupled from the rear of an eastward train inside tunnel and proceed in the opposite direction. Protection as per Rule 99 is not required within these limits.

The west siding switch at East Portal (located immediately inside the Moffat Tunnel) is lever controlled by fan operator. Eastward movements over this switch are governed by Dwarf Signal 502 (two signals) located five (5) feet west of switch. The top signal governs movements on main track; lower signal governs restricted movements through turnout to siding. All signals governing movements over this switch, in addition to their ABS function, will not indicate "Proceed" or "Approach" unless ventilation curtain is raised.

Eastward Signal 504 (located inside tunnel 900 feet west of Signal 502) repeats indication of signal 502 by displaying green when upper signal 502 displays green or yellow, and yellow when upper signal 502 displays red. Signal 504 will not display "Stop" indication.

Dwarf Signal 531 (a two-color signal—red and yellow), located at Refuge 9, governs westward helper engine movements backing out of tunnel. The signal is normally dark for through westward movement and when not illuminated will not govern such through movements. If signal indicates "Stop," engine or train will stop and then proceed at a speed not exceeding five (5) miles per hour.

White flashing light signals for information regarding proximity of tunnel portals are located—one for westward trains at Refuge No. 21 and one for eastward trains 1750 feet west of the east portal.

Eastward trains must not exceed a speed of ten (10) miles per hour or consume less than two minutes from a point 1750 feet west of ventilation curtain until train has cleared tunnel. Eastward freight trains must stop at East Portal and will not exceed this speed before stop is made. Maximum grade between the apex (MP 52.8) and Winter Park is 0.9%, descending westward. Maximum grade east from the apex is 0.3%, descending eastward to 650 feet east of tunnel portal where it increases to 2%. When engine of an eastward freight train has arrived at the 2% grade, engineman must exercise care to insure stopping train clear of west switch. It is unsafe to make more than one application of brakes in making this stop.

Motor cars, other than trains, must obtain, from the dispatcher through the operator at Winter Park, authority on Form 1223-R before occupying or passing through the Moffat Tunnel.

A switch which operates a bell in ventilating plant is located on south side of tunnel fifteen (15) feet west of curtain, by means of which fan operator may be signaled that curtain is to be raised.

Telephones in Moffat Tunnel.

Refuge No.	M.P.	Refuge No.	M.P.
1	50.6	9	53.0
3	51.2	11	53.3
4	51.5	13	53.7
7	52.4	16	54.4
8	52.7	18	54.8
Apex	52.8	19	55.3

These telephones connect with telegraph office, Winter Park, and Ventilating Plant, East Portal, and may be connected with dispatching circuits at these stations. They operate with hand ringing generators, four long rings for East Portal, one short, one long, one short ring for Winter Park and a succession of long rings quickly repeated must be promptly answered by both East Portal and Winter Park.

Other refuges have no telephones.

Each engine in a train must have maximum steam pressure and fire in good condition before train enters tunnel so as to reduce firing to the minimum after entry. If necessary to insure this, train should be stopped outside tunnel for conditioning of engine. ELIMINATE SMOKE.

Operate engine stack hood in deflecting position at all times inside the tunnel while throttle is open. It must be in deflecting position while passing under curtain at East Portal, eastward or westward. Engineman on westward trains must operate deflector not less than 50 feet from the curtain.

Operate engine blower throughout tunnel, and if engine is equipped with air cooling jets in cab, operate them while engine is working in tunnel.

If excessive heat is developed in the train, it is apt to be occasioned by insufficient train speed and this is particularly true in the case of westward trains. Increase speed within the maximum permissible, if possible, and endeavor to run out of the hot zone. If this cannot be done within a minute or two, stop train and communicate promptly with fan operator by nearest refuge telephone.

If an engine is used to shove a westward train into the tunnel, do not shove beyond ABS 501 or ABS 501-A.

If a train stops in the tunnel for any reason, except to uncouple helper engine at the Apex, fan operator should be promptly notified from nearest refuge telephone of the reason for the stop.

6-G. Operation Through All Tunnels—Windows, vestibule doors, connecting doors and other openings must be closed and air conditioning apparatus shut off on all passenger trains moving through tunnels.

A 9000-horsepower trio of SD40T-2s (5343-5355-5353) leads an empty coal train up to East Portal, enroute to the same northwestern Colorado coal fields that were the goal of the Denver Northwestern & Pacific 70 years earlier. These units have specially designed air intakes and radiators for more efficient operation in the many tunnels of this route. *(left)* The *Rio Grande Zephyr* finds a brief sanctuary from a Rocky Mountain blizzard of December 1977; in about ten minutes it will emerge at Winter Park. A Moffat train in pre-tunnel days would have faced a far greater battle on a day such as this. Below, a fast Rio Grande freight bursts from the west portal with merchandise bound from the Midwest to the Pacific Coast. A picture taken at this same spot 40 years before is at the top of page forty. (center, Mel Patrick; others, Ronald C. Hill)

The silence of a winter day at East Portal is broken by the whine of dynamic brakes as tunnel motor 5356 leads a unit coal train toward Denver. (Mel Patrick photo) In the 1970s, the *Rio Grande Zephyr* became the last of a long line of D&RGW trains. No. 18 slips into the west portal of the tunnel in the dying light of a late June afternoon in 1973. It is perhaps David Moffat's most lasting tribute that even today this portion of the railroad is known as "the Moffat line." (left, Ted Benson photo)

Railroad artist Howard Fogg had a Rio Grande cab permit. At the top, he photographed an Alco PA on the *Yampa Valley Mail* emerging at East Portal. On another occasion in the late 1950s, when solid sets of GP9s were used as mainline freight power, he recorded a train entering the tunnel. A fireman's view of East Portal shows some of the fill composed of excavated tunnel rock. (Howard Fogg photos, CRRM collection)

Several hundred people, most of whom had come up on the *Rio Grande Zephyr*, huddle around East Portal on the snowy morning of February 25, 1978, for the golden anniversary of the Moffat Tunnel when the time capsule was opened. The following summer a new capsule was placed in the portal's facade by the Intermountain Chapter of the National Railway Historical Society, to be opened in February 2028. (Charles Albi photo)

Later in the day, U.S. Postal Clerk Jim Brairton dispatches mail from the commemorative Denver & Salt Lake RPO to Bond, Colorado, Postmaster Iva C. Seaman. (Ronald Hill photo) Above is one of the special postal cachets issued by the NRHS. Over 80,000 pieces of mail were handled by the February 25-26 Railway Post Office. (Kenton Forrest collection)

How many trains have penetrated the Moffat's darkness since 1928? The classic facade of the east portal looms over the waiting train and dwarfs the people gathered to remember the achievement of the dream of one of Colorado's most famous citizens, David Halliday Moffat. In the background, falling snow engulfs the silent mountains. (Charles Albi photo)

(above) NRHS National President V. Allan Vaughn addresses the crowd during the 50th Anniversary ceremonies. Behind him are several of the tunnel commissioners and representatives of the D&RGW and the Colorado Railroad Historical Foundation. (above right) As the *Rio Grande Zephyr* goes through the Moffat Tunnel, officials, guests and crew listen to Alexis McKinney talk about the life of David Moffat. (right) CRHF trustees Roy Altenbach and Charles Albi hold the new and old plaques prior to resealing the time capsule in August 1978. (Ronald C. Hill photos)

After 13 years of running what had become the last privately owned intercity passenger train in the United States, D&RGW in early 1983 decided to allow Amtrak to replace the by then world famous *Rio Grande Zephyr.* A trial run of Superliner equipment was made on one *RGZ* round trip to Salt Lake City and is seen here entering the Moffat on February 7, witnessed only by the photographer and a small section crew.

Meanwhile, work continued on revamping of the ventilation system at East Portal, assisted by this GP40-2 and a caboose of the style that had served the Moffat Tunnel Route for over 40 years. (all, John Sherman photos)

The Moffat Tunnel has entered the new era of railroad mergers. Denver & Rio Grande Western combined with Southern Pacific in 1988; then in 1996 SP was acquired by Union Pacific. At that time, Burlington Northern Santa Fe acquired trackage rights between Denver and Salt Lake City. *(top)* Westbound SP 8118 and 8119 are in Denver-Granby helper service on June 7, 1994. (Wesley Fox photo) An eastbound BNSF freight emerges from the tunnel on October 1, 1999. In a few weeks, the mountain behind it will be white with snow. (Ronald Hill photo). On March 30, 2001, Mike Danneman photographed the eastbound *Ski Train (below)* at East Portal with newly painted F40PH units.

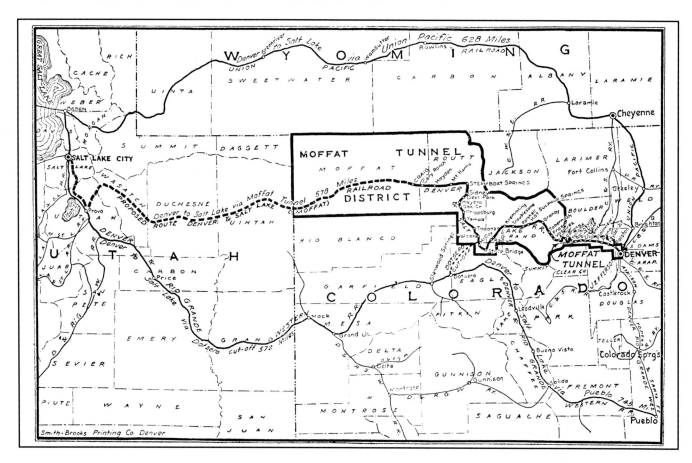

This map of the Moffat Tunnel Improvement District also shows the area along the Denver & Rio Grande Western mainline that was benefited after completion of the Dotsero Cutoff in1934 without having to pay the Moffat Tunnel tax. Comparative Denver-Salt Lake City mileages were 628 via the Union Pacific, 745 via the D&RGW Pueblo line, 578 via the never completed D&SL extension and 572 via the Dotsero Cutoff. (Moffat Tunnel Commission)

PASSENGER TRAINS THAT HAVE OPERATED THROUGH THE MOFFAT TUNNEL

Number	Name	Route	Dates
D&SL 1-2	-- --	Denver - Craig	2/26/28 - 4/10/47
D&RGW 5-6	*Panoramic*	Denver - Salt Lake City	6/17/34 - 9/24/39
D&SL 11-12	-- --	Denver - Craig	1/15/36(?)- 4/10/47
D&RGW 19-20	*Mountaineer*	Denver - Montrose	7/05/36 - 10/24/59
D&RGW 5-6	*Exposition Flyer*	Chicago - San Francisco	6/11/39 - 3/20/49
D&RGW 7-8	*Prospector*	Denver - Salt Lake City	11/17/41 - 7/04/42
D&RGW 8	*Advance Exposition Flyer*	Salt Lake City - Denver	1/16/44 - 10/13/45
D&RGW 7	*Advance Exposition Flyer*	Denver - Salt Lake City	5/13/45 - 10/13/45
D&RGW 7-8	*Prospector*	Denver - Salt Lake City	10/14/45 - 5/28/67
D&RGW 23-24	-- --	Denver - Craig	4/11/47 - 12.31.50
D&RGW 9-10	-- --	Denver - Craig	4/11/47 - 12.31.50
D&RGW 17-18	*California Zephyr*	Chicago - San Francisco	3/21/49 - 3/21/70
D&RGW 9-10	*Yampa Valley Mail*	Denver - Craig	9/05/54 - 10/31/63
D&RGW 9-10	*Yampa Valley*	Denver - Craig	11/01/63 - 4/07/68
D&RGW 17-18	*Rio Grande Zephyr*	Denver - Salt Lake City	3/22/70 - 4/24/83
Amtrak 5-6	*California Zephyr*	Chicago - San Francisco	7/16/83 - Present